Practical English
Summercamp Activities

Practical English Summercamp Activities

Barry Nicholson

Starhands Publishing

Practical English Summercamp Activities

Copyright © 2015 Barry Nicholson. All rights reserved.
First paperback edition printed 2015.

A catalogue record for this book is available from the British Library.

ISBN: 9780993243806
ISBN: 0993243800

No part of this book shall be reproduced or transmitted in any form or by any means, electronic or mechanical, including photocopying, recording, or by any information retrieval system without written permission of the publisher.

Published by Starhands Publishing
www.starhandspublishing.co.uk

Printed in the United States

Although every precaution has been taken in the preparation of this book, the publisher and author assume no responsibility for errors or omissions. Neither is any liability assumed for damages resulting from the use of this information contained herein.

Introduction
Welcome to Summer Camp!

Summer camps and extracurricular classes are by nature interactive and fun. The activities in this book are aimed at primary-aged learners who speak English as their second language (ESL). The material is designed to provide appropriate activities that will help students learn and apply the English language in a fun and creative environment.

A typical summer (or winter) camp might last one or two weeks and have classroom-based lessons and activities in the morning and sports or excursions in the afternoon. There may even be evening sessions for journal writing or watching a film if the children are to stay overnight. It is important to create a cheerful and cooperative atmosphere and a time to make new friends and explore English in an informal and relaxed environment. A far cry from the usual routine of textbooks and blackboard!

Let's think for a moment about the importance of being active, of participation in the context of the classroom. That's how the activities in this book fit into a summer camp or extracurricular lesson, and that's what leads to learning.

Barry Nicholson

The Importance of Being Active

Picture yourself in a class of forty students listening to a prerecorded tape and answering questions and marking off multiple-choice answers in their workbooks. A, B, C, or D? Just A, B, C, and D—that's all they're learning. Their pencil only touches the paper to write A, B, C, or D. How boring. How passive.

You don't learn much this way, except the first four letters of the alphabet! What you really need is participation—active participation. For a start you need a smaller group—fifteen at most—and a good, confident teacher who can control the children (and not vice versa!). Then you need to actively involve the children in their learning experience by getting them to do things, say things, and remember things. Bring back creativity to the classroom! Where did it go?

Each child is independent, and of course one cannot spend the whole time pampering to each child's need. But grouped together as an effective class you have golddust; manage them and involve them and let them have some fun within this firm and predetermined structure.

In this book I stress the importance of the following formula:

Active Fun + Learning = Success

This works! Set it up properly, execute it properly, and watch the growing glow on the children's faces from lesson to lesson. It is the children who are important. By being active, the children you teach will gain a fortune of knowledge as never before presented to them through a more traditional medium.

"Traditional" classes do have their place, of course, but active classes are so much more rewarding and in many cases need less preparation. More importantly, they get everyone off their seat and actually doing something. Active classes are easy! Which is it for you? A, B, C, or D?

The Following Activities as Part of a Lesson

Languages do not have to be boring! Children often learn more through fun activities than through traditional teaching techniques. So this is a book of fun educational activities.

If one remembers the English Teacher's Pyramid of 1) presentation, 2) practice, and 3) further practice, one can see that the latter two segments refer to this book. In effect, then, it is a collection of student transfer activities. The first presentation stage (vocabulary, sentence patterns, etc.) is left to the teacher.

These activities form part of the lesson. They are the more active part—the fun plus the learning part. Use the activities as you will, but it is highly recommended to use them within the P-P-P pyramid above.

This Book

The book itself is divided as follows:

1. Introduction Activities—useful for the first lesson or as icebreakers
2. Classic Primary Activities—tried and tested, these will go down well in any situation
3. Other Activities—perhaps a little more offbeat or restricted
4. Paper Activities—a lot of active activities with the use of paper

I trust this book provides a valuable source of information and, more importantly, ideas for your lesson plans. Remember, participation is the key: one must be active instead of passive, enthusiastic instead of boring. Most of all, have fun!

Barry Nicholson
Hong Kong 1996

Table of Contents

Introduction
Welcome to Summer Camp! · v
The Importance of Being Active · · · · · · · · · · · · · · · · · ·vi
The Following Activities as Part of a Lesson · · · · · · · · · · · vii
This Book· ·viii

Part 1
Introduction Activities· 1

A Fish for Names· 3
A Names Lucky Dip· 4
Ball Throw · 5
Name Badges · 6
Something Interesting· 7
Vocabulary Dictionary · 8

Part 2
Classic Primary Activities· 9

Anybody Who's? · 11
Bingo · 12
Birthday Party· 14

Blindfold Obstacle Course · 16
Board Rush · 18
Body Annotation · 19
Change! · 20
Circle Drills · 21
Follow the Leader · 22
Group Rush · 24
Guess Who? · 25
Guess Who? (Gestures) · 26
Hangman · 27
Is It You? · 28
Karaoke · 29
Kim's Game · 31
Lucky Dip · 32
Mime Game · 33
Musical Statues · 34
Progressive Memory Game · · · · · · · · · · · · · · · · · · · 35
Simon Says · 36
Simon Says (Variations) · 37
Statues · 39
What's He (or She) Doing Now? · · · · · · · · · · · · · · 41

Part 3
Other Primary Activities · 43

Balloon Volleyball · 44
Bottle Spin · 45
Brick-Stack Game · 46
Cardboard Rocket · 48
Colour Collecting · 50
Crash · 51
Dressing-Up Race · 52
Egyptian Mummy · 53

Famous Person Quiz	55
Fancy Dress Party	57
Feel Bags	58
Golden Bell	60
Good, Horrid, In-Between	61
Hunt the Thimble	62
Jeopardy Quiz	63
Letters Lucky Dip	65
Letter Sort	67
Measurement—Parts of the Body	68
Measurement—Height Line-Up	69
Mingle Survey—Questionnaire	71
Murals	73
Pass the Parcel	74
Percussion Band	75
Pin the Tail on the Dinosaur	76
Pronunciation Mingle	77
Raise Your Left Leg…	78
Role Plays	80
Scavenger Hunt	82
Seeds and Plants	83
Shout Out!	85
Sink or Float?	86
Simple Exercises	88
Skittles	89
Stage Plays	90
Target Practice (Bucket Throw)	92
Time Acting	93
Time and Big Ben	94
Tongue Twisters	95
Twenty Questions	96
Twister	97
Word Associations	99

Part 4
Paper Activities · 101

ABC Words · 103
Anagrams · 104
A Word Beginning With… · 105
Blindfold Drawing · 106
Body Construction · 107
Collages · 108
Constantinople · 109
Creative Badges · 110
Crosswords · 111
Describe and Draw · 112
Dot-to-Dot · 113
Journal Writing · 114
Making Books · 116
Matching Exercise · 118
Paper Football Pitch · 120
Paper Puzzle · 121
Pelmanism · 122
Picture Description · 123
Picture Gap-Fill · 125
Poem Construction · 126
Sentence Construction · 128
Snap! · 130
Sound Snap! · 131
Spot the Difference · 132
Stories from Words · 133
Treasure Chest and Money · · · · · · · · · · · · · · · · · · 134
Word Chart · 135
Word Circle · 136
Word Figure of Eight · 137
Word Search · 138

Part 5
Sample Lessons · 139

Introduction Lesson ·141
Parts of the Body· ·143
Giving Directions ·144
Going Shopping ·145
Postscript ·146
About the Author ·149

Part I
Introduction Activities

It stands to reason that a class works better once everyone's got to know each other. One must break the ice in the first lesson, but also one must consider practical things, like giving children English names or taking the register (roll call). Of course, one has to let the children know who's boss in the first lesson, but within this framework there is plenty of scope for "controlled fun" and getting to know each other.

Practical English Summercamp Activities

A Fish for Names

Level: Primary 1–4

Time taken: 15 minutes

Introduction

I consider it very important to give English names to those students without, especially at the primary level. This is one of the many methods of doing so in a more practical and creative way.

Method

Put a large bucket, or similar such container, in the middle of the room and gather your students around it. Taking turns, students without English names "fish" for a name from the bucket using a toy net or magnetic device attached to a stick. Don't forget to find names for the girls and the boys separately (or the children will not be happy!).

A Names Lucky Dip

Level: Primary 1–6

Time taken: 15 minutes

Introduction

This is similar to fishing for names and is also used as a fun and practical first activity.

Method

Write a selection of boys' and girls' names on cards, and place them in a bucket or bag. The girls and boys take their names separately. I suggest you line the children up until they take a name. After they take a name, they can quietly sit down. The name cards can be pegged on with ordinary clothes pegs.

Lucky dips are always a good choice if you are stuck for something to do, as they can be adapted into so many different situations.

Ball Throw

Level: Primary 1–6

Time taken: 10–15 minutes

Introduction

If all your students have their English names you can play this fun activity, guaranteed to put a smile on every child's face. It is also an excellent way of getting to know each other's name.

Method

Sit or stand in a circle. Throw a soft toy or ball to each other, calling out your own name as you go. You can throw the ball to anyone you like—not necessarily in order. This will introduce each child's name to the whole group.

After you have done this for a while, you can go on to the next stage: say the name of the person you throw the ball to! This is bound to be difficult at first, especially if you take away the students' name badges.

Name Badges

Level: Primary 1–6

Time taken: 10–15 minutes

Introduction

To aid efficiency in the classroom, it is a good idea to make name badges for each student. This will be particularly important in the first few lessons when you will still be unfamiliar with names.

Method

The children will probably enjoy making their own name badges using the English names they picked before. Use colourful cards, and clearly instruct the children to write in *big* letters. The name badge can be attached with a clothes peg.

Depending on your creativity level, you can spend as much time as you want making the badges. Whatever they look like, they will help you remember names and drill "introductions" more effectively.

Something Interesting

Level: Primary 5–6

Time taken: 20 minutes

Introduction

Getting to know something about each other is important in the initial stages, and this activity is designed to allow students to say something about themselves and their interests. It allows for "freetalk" within a firm structure.

Method

Draw a line down the middle of the board. The children, one by one, write their name on the left-hand side and something important or good for them on the right (e.g., football, money, an expensive car, etc.). You may have to demonstrate to give them the idea.

Once this is done, you can go on to the second stage—go around the class and see if the children can remember who is connected with each thing. Extend this by asking the students in question why these things are important—a chance to share information through freetalk.

Vocabulary Dictionary

❖ ❖ ❖

Level: Primary 1–6

Time taken: 15–20 minutes

Introduction

Within the context of any course, it is useful to keep a note of all new words encountered. Instead of referring to a well-thumbed class dictionary, why not make one of your own?

Method

If you can afford it, give each child a separate notebook, which becomes their dictionary. Get the children to write their name clearly on the front, plus the word "Dictionary" or "Word Book." Following your instruction, the children go through the pages writing A on the first page, B on the second, and so on. Now they have the "skeleton" of their dictionary; the "muscle" comes with the words they add throughout the course.

Make sure each child updates his or her dictionary at the end of each class. Let them decorate it in whichever way they want. They should learn to cherish their book and value its importance—don't let it become a chore.

Part 2
Classic Primary Activities

There is a whole host of activities that can be used almost anytime you want, in any situation. These are what I call the Classic Primary Activities. Quite a few of them you will have come across before, perhaps at children's parties. But have you ever considered using them in the classroom? They are guaranteed to raise a smile everytime!

Anybody Who's?

❖ ❖ ❖

Level: Primary 1–6

Time taken: 20 minutes

Introduction

Adaptable activities are often the best and in common with many of those presented in this book Anybody Who's can be used in an unusually large range of situations. In common with the Board Rush, it combines education with physical exercise.

Method

Arrange several chairs in a circle, for the students to sit on, with one or two seats to spare. With the chosen topic in mind, call out something to which only certain students can respond. Those students then change seats with each other. For example, the chosen subject might be colours of clothes; if the teacher calls out, "Anyone who's wearing blue," then all students wearing blue clothes swap seats. A mad rush will ensue, but the children will seem strangely focussed on the activity and will be eager to sit in their new places quickly and wait for the next instruction.

Other topics that work well are physical features (long hair, big nose, etc.), people who live in a particular place, and so on.

Bingo

❖ ❖ ❖

Level: Primary 3–6

Time taken: 15 minutes

Introduction

Well known in England as an old-age pensioner's favourite pastime, this activity is also well applied to society's younger members. It can be used in a wealth of situations. You might find that the students don't understand the idea of the game at first, so be patient.

Method

It is possible to use a number of topics with your game of Bingo, but the most well-known game is the version with numbers.

Make a board of squares—four by four is best—which can be copied a number of times. Write the numbers one to ten at random in the squares. Give one board to each team of three or four. Pick out numbered cards from a Lucky Dip bag or basket, call them out, and get the teams to mark the number off their board. When a team crosses off a line of four on the board, it is the winner—and the team should shout, "Bingo!" Then you can continue with the first team to cross off the four corners of the grid then to cross off all numbers on the grid.

One of my favourite variations is Opposites Bingo. Instead of numbers, write opposites on your grid and in your Lucky Dip bag. This turns the activity into a thinking activity.

Birthday Party

❖ ❖ ❖

Level: Primary 1–6

Time taken: 10-plus minutes

Introduction

When is your birthday? Children love parties, and it need not be a birthday party—it could be a New Year's party, end-of-term party, congratulations party, successful-completion-of-your-summer-camp party, and so on. A party will put a smile on any child's face—especially a surprise party.

Method

It takes a bit of forward planning, but it's worth it. There are some classic items that one would expect: cake, soda, paper hats, lively music, and some party games.

Cakes come in all sizes and can vary from expensive in style (from a cake shop) down to cheap and cheerful (homemade). I have found it best to buy a cake base and to let the children decorate it with cream, yoghurt, pretty decorative sprinkles, and some candles. It's probably best for the teacher to light the candles and cut the cake, for safety reasons.

Soda can be bought cheaply and poured into individual plastic cups. Again, this might be a job for the teacher or a reliable student. Paper hats are easy to make: Cut an A4 paper in half, and cut a zigzag edge into it. Staple or stick the two halves together. Lively music is essential, especially if you are going to play one of the party games such as Pass the Parcel or Musical Statues.

Blindfold Obstacle Course

Level: Primary 1–6

Time taken: 15–20 minutes

Introduction

Many blindfold games for primary-age children exist. This one is a more unusual variation but, at the same time, quite simplistic. Be careful, though, to control this activity well. The activity fits in well to a lesson on directions.

Method

Make sure from the outset that the students know the difference between left, right, and straight ahead, all basic ingredients for this activity.

Arrange the room or playground so that some obstacles (tables, chairs, etc.) restrict the way from one side to the other. In turn, students are blindfolded to be directed by the others through this maze. The other students will become very enthusiastic about shouting out directions, which is where your teacher control comes in; calm them down, and make them give directions in English!

An added incentive would be to make the goal a chocolate bar or sweet; even the most passive children will go through with the activity in order to get their reward!

Board Rush

Level: Primary 1–6

Time taken: 20 minutes

Introduction

Sometimes activities combine thinking with physical exercise, as is so with Board Rush. Teamwork is also important in this fun and practical activity that is good for review of previously taught vocabulary.

Method

Divide the class into two teams, lined up on either side of the blackboard. Give the first child in each team a chalk to write with. Upon you saying some stimulus, the two people at the front of the lines compete to write it down first or most accurately. Give the teams points as you see fit. The difficulty can be increased by just having one chalk, or by having the children construct sentences from the word. You could also include the stimulus words within a short story to increase difficulty.

Organization is the key with this activity—students must know who's boss or the whole thing might degenerate into a frenzied cloud of chalk! Ensure order from the outset.

Body Annotation

Level: Primary 1–6

Time taken: 15–20 minutes

Introduction

Children seem fascinated by parts of the body—mention "nose" and they will laugh! The following is a good way of consolidating the names of parts of the body, and it works well with a classic body song such as "Head, Shoulders, Knees and Toes."

Method

Choose a person to be a "body," or if you feel this is too adventurous, draw a large body figure on the board. Write the names of various parts of the body on pieces of paper or cards and put them into a Lucky Dip bag. Students take it in turns to pull out a card and stick it to the "body." After a while the "body" will be covered in about twenty little pieces of paper, all correctly naming the body parts.

You must remember a couple of things. First, don't make your body parts too obscure—adapt them according to ability. Second, have consideration for the "body"—sometimes students get annoyed with people sticking bits of paper all over them. But if you do this activity well, you will become very popular!

Change!

Level: Primary 1–4

Time taken: 10 minutes

Introduction

Both active and fun, you can breathe a lot of new life into a conservative class with this simple activity.

Method

The children stand in a circle, close enough together to pass an object around. Indeed, this is the idea—just to pass some object around (such as a ball or soft toy). However, when the teacher clearly says "Change!" the object must reverse and be passed in the other direction. Make this complicated by calling "Change!" numerous times—you'll soon pick up the simple tricks of when to call. If your students are sufficiently advanced, one of them can call "Change!"

A simple adaptation of this is to call "Left!" or "Right!" or even "Across!"

Circle Drills

Level: Primary 1–6

Time taken: 10–20 minutes

Introduction

Circle drills are good activities as they can be used in almost any situation with any topic. Children say and learn words or questions and answers without realizing it, and fun can be shared all around.

Method

The children stand in a circle or around a large table. Some word or sentence is then "passed" around the circle. This could be just one word, or it might take the form of a question and answer. So, for example, the first child could say to the next, "What is your name?" and the second child would reply, "My name is Sam", then the second child would ask the third, and so on.

A Complex Circle Drill is an adaptation of the above, and much more fun. Instead of having one word or sentence passed around, have two—but make them go in opposite directions. One poor child will have words or questions coming from both sides *at the same time*!

Follow the Leader

Level: Primary 1–3

Time taken: 15 minutes

Introduction

Children love to imitate each other and this activity allows them to do so in a fun and practical way.

Method

One student is the leader and moves around the room with the others following conga-style. As the leader moves, he or she dances and makes movements with his or her arms or legs and the other children must copy this. For example, if the leader dances from side to side and raises his or her left leg the students behind must do the same. The leader can change the dance as often as he or she likes.

Most students will be able to follow the leader well, but some will be late to copy the new dance the leader is making. In any case the results can be very comical, and the procession continues until a new leader is selected.

Practical English Summercamp Activities

Group Rush

Level: Primary 1–4

Time taken: 10 minutes

Introduction

Children with lower levels of English will delight in this fun and practical activity. Its educational value is questionable, however, and relies heavily on the consolidation of three or four key words.

Method

You will need a large open area free of all obstructions (or best Sunday china). A large class of around fifteen to twenty children also helps.

Write four key words in large clear letters on four separate papers. Position one child at each of the four sides of the room, each clearly holding up one of the key words. The other children stand in the middle. Simply, on calling out one of the key words, the children rush to the child holding that word. Alternate children and key words as you go, but don't let the children become too noisy and carefree!

Guess Who?

Level: Primary 1–6

Time taken: 20 minutes

Introduction

"Does your person with a hat wear glasses?" You might be familiar with this game in which one has to guess the opponent's "person" from many choices. This is a good game, especially when teaching about personal facial description. However, for group teaching, I prefer a simple variation of the standard game.

Method

A "Guess Who?" set consists of twenty-four characters, each with differing facial features. One student secretly picks a card; the others must ask questions about the facial features of the person, and then attempt to draw the person based on the information they have. When the "real" person is placed next to the students' attempts, hilarious scenes are caused!

If you really get to grips with your set of twenty-four characters, you can make several variations of your own. One of my favourites, good with a larger class, is to make the children themselves the "people"—a good way to personalize this valuable game.

Guess Who? (Gestures)

Level: Primary 1–4

Time taken: 10–15 minutes

Introduction

When I started teaching, this was the first game I came across, funnily enough taught to me by my primary students! It involves the whole group, is practical, and above all is great fun.

Method

The game itself is similar to Follow the Leader, except it involves gestures whilst sitting down. One child is sent out of the room. While he or she is out, one person is selected as the leader. The leader is the person whom the other students will follow. He or she makes gestures for the others to copy (e.g., clapping, waving arms, tapping a foot). The child who was sent out comes back in and must guess who the leader is—watch this child's face, full of concentration! When the leader is found, he or she is the next to go out of the room while a new leader is chosen.

Hangman

Level: Primary 5–6

Time taken: 20 minutes

Introduction

This is another popular game that I suspect most of us have come across in some shape or form. It's not only good for a review of ABCs but also because it can be related to any topic.

Method

Students must guess the word or phrase before they are "hung." Write dashes on the board according to the number of letters in the word. In turn, students guess letters. If guessed correctly, the letter is added on top of the appropriate dash; if not, a crossbeam is added to the frame for example. The students must guess the word before the frame and man are completed.

Whoever correctly guesses the word can be "teacher" in the next round (while you take a rest). This activity is immensely popular and can be played time and time again without fear of boredom.

Barry Nicholson

Is It You?

Level: Primary 1–6

Time taken: 15 minutes

Introduction

A guessing game with a difference, this activity connects well with a lesson about objects—like things found in the classroom (ruler, pencil case, etc.). The whole class can join in, usually with great enthusiasm.

Method

Choose an object, like a book, which is clearly shown to all pupils. One child is sent out of the room whilst the object is hidden with one of the other pupils. The first child is then called back into the room and has to guess which classmate has the object hidden on him or her. The child points and asks, "Is it you?" This continues until he or she correctly guesses who has the object. The child who had the object is sent out, and the game carries on as before.

Increase the difficulty by asking the remaining students to secretly move the object around about themselves—the object is always on the move, and so is the guessing! You can have a turn at guessing, too!

Karaoke

Level: Primary 1–6

Time taken: 20 minutes

Introduction

Singing is a big pleasure, especially for children! Songs can affect our mood, be it a slow lullaby to sleep or a jig designed to make us get up and dance. Words together with music is also a combination of fun (singing) with learning (words in order and context).

Method

The best way to start is to choose an easy song depending on the age of the students. For very young students, try "Old MacDonald" or "London Bridge Is Falling Down." Older students may enjoy a simple pop song (try a golden oldies 60s or 70s compilation for ideas).

It is a good idea to drill the song first. You can either do this directly, as in listen and repeat, or indirectly as in a gap-fill or sentence-ordering exercise. If you have a tape of the song, that's even better. Students can then split into groups to practice the lyrics and melody until they are reasonably happy. Ask for a group to volunteer to be the first to perform in front of their classmates. Offer a prize for the best as incentive!

Kim's Game

Level: Primary 1–6

Time taken: 10–15 minutes

Introduction

Can you remember all the things you did yesterday? If one of these things was wiped from your memory, could you deduce what it was? Memory is an important skill. If you can't remember where you are or what you were going to do next, you are lost!

Method

Collect a number of small objects, possibly based around a theme. Place the objects on a table and run through what they are. Place a cloth or towel over the things and carefully take one (or more) objects away. Remove the cloth and see if the students can figure out which thing is missing—chances are they won't be able to at first, but they'll soon remember the lot without fail. You can joke with your students by removing all the objects, or by adding an object. Don't forget to let them have a go at being "teacher."

Lucky Dip

❖ ❖ ❖

Level: Primary 1–6

Time taken: 10–15 minutes

Introduction

You will be familiar with this activity, famed for its mystery and element of surprise. You just never know what you will pull out of the bag! Here, an outline of the activity is given, followed by a couple of variations of it.

Method

You can use one of two things for your lucky dip—either a bag or box (possibly filled with torn-up paper or small lumps of polystyrene to conceal the objects).

Traditionally, the Lucky Dip bag consists of a number of objects that the children take turns pulling out of the bag. Some of the things are valuable and worthy, whilst others are insignificant and hardly worth the effort.

There is a variation of this that is more suited to teaching: instead of using objects, use pieces of paper with some written stimulus on them—perhaps vocabulary or sentences relating to your chosen topic such as a body parts Lucky dip (see Body Annotation). Another variation would be to have some task or forfeit written on the papers.

Mime Game

Level: Primary 1–6

Time taken: 10–15 minutes

Introduction

This is one of the simplest and most straightforward of all the activities in this book, and it's quite fundamental as it helps the children acquire acting skills. Moreover, they must use their imagination and gain enough confidence to stand at the centre of the class.

Method

As the name tells you, this is acting out some stimulus according to the chosen topic. Such topics might be, for example, animals, jobs in the home, or famous people.

Students take turns coming to the front of the class and acting out an animal (for example). You might wish to give the students freedom of choice, you could assign an animal according to their ability level, or you could include an element of chance by putting things into a Lucky Dip bag or facedown on the table. The amount of control is up to you, but whichever method, the children gain confidence as they mime successive times. But you might have to give them the idea of it by acting the things out first.

Musical Statues

Level: Primary 1–4

Time taken: 15 minutes

Introduction

This is similar to statues, but it requires the extra prop of a tape recorder plus lively music.

Method

The children stand about in the room, dancing to your music. However, when the music stops, they must again stand stock-still. Go around and tease them, making them sit out if they move. Encourage them to dance wildly while the music is playing (itself a game) and give them a second or two to stand still after the music stops.

Progressive Memory Game

Level: Primary 3–4

Time taken: 10–15 minutes

Introduction

The act of remembering is an important skill tested in this potentially never-ending activity. It teaches something further about memory—that things are more easily remembered in sequence.

Method

Decide on the topic to use, popularly something along the lines of shopping or ordering food. Get the students into some sort of order, most preferably a circle. Start the game by saying, "I went shopping and I bought…" The next person must recite this and also add something to the list. The next person must recite all the things on the list and add something of his or her own, and so on. You will end up with a long shopping list that's unwieldy and difficult to remember—especially in the correct order.

Simon Says

Level: Primary 1–6

Time taken: 15 minutes

Introduction

This is a well-known children's activity, not least because they are actively and practically involved at all times. They are required to concentrate on the instructions given and react only to certain instructions and not others. If done well, Simon Says gives group participation new meaning.

Method

When Simon Says something, the children must do it; an instruction given that Simon does not "say" must be ignored. The teacher calls the instructions. For example, upon the instruction "Simon says stand up," all children must stand up. However, upon the instruction "put your hands on your head," the children must not obey ("Simon" did not say anything). Try instructions such as stand up; sit down; put your hands on your head, nose, or tummy; turn around; stand on one leg; and so on.

Simon Says (Variations)

Level: Primary 1–6

Time taken: 15 minutes

Introduction

Whilst fundamentally similar to Simon Says, the variations take the activity into a new dimension. Try these and you will become popular!

Method

Once the children have the hang of Simon Says, ask one of them to be "Simon." This can be quite amusing, but you will frequently have to help "Simon." Watch out for and steer clear of ridiculous instructions, such as "Simon says stand on your table."

There is another extremely effective adaptation, which strays a little from Simon Says into physical exercises. Hold up a pen, for example, and say, "Simon says point to the pen" (be patient as they may have difficulty in understanding "point"). When all the children are pointing at the pen, move it slowly from left to right or up and down. Watch their faces as they realize that they are starting to perform physical exercises. Go even further—walk around the room with the children still pointing at the object, or even introduce a "Simon says stand on one leg" and then walk around the room, children still pointing! Once, as a teacher, you get the hang of this, you can adapt the technique in so many ways, or even make a whole lesson out of it.

Statues

Level: Primary 1–4

Time taken: 15 minutes

Introduction

Have you ever tried to stand completely still for any amount of time? As you can imagine, such an act requires the utmost coordination and concentration. Challenge the children to do this with this simple and popular game.

Method

Stand the children in a line at one side of a room or playground. Go to the other side of this area and turn your back to the children. When your back is turned, the children must cautiously move towards you. But when you turn and look at them, the children must stand stock-still. Any who are not are sent back to the starting line.

Aggravate the children by staring them in the face, waving your arms at them, or by pulling funny faces. Try to make them move! You will find that some are amazingly good at standing still and expressionless; others will titter or collapse with laughter at the first sign of you teasing them.

Good fun is had all around, but you must remember to enforce the rules of the game tightly as an ill-disciplined class will murder its simple beauty.

What's He (or She) Doing Now?

Level: Primary 1–4

Time taken: 10 minutes

Introduction

This is a variation of the Mime Game activity, but it's more limited in scope. It cannot obviously be connected to any topic except for the phonic sound "ou," but it serves well as a gap filler or warmer.

Method

Pupils take turns miming one of the following activities, all with a similar "ou" sound:

1. Sitting down
2. Lying down
3. Running around
4. Shouting
5. Clowning around

The others must try to guess what the first is doing. Each time the teacher asks, "What's he (or she) doing now?" the students have to reply "He's (or she's)…" Use prompt cards for the mimes if you want.

Part 3
Other Primary Activities

Some activities are a little offbeat or restricted in nature. This does not mean to say that they are any less useful, but as a teacher you might have to think a bit more as to where the activity will go within your lesson.

It is worth pointing out that so many of these activities can be adapted to your own teaching style—and in many cases you can make up your own games based on the ideas presented here.

Balloon Volleyball

Level: Primary 1–3

Time taken: 20 minutes

Introduction

This is a variation of the usual court volleyball, not especially educational, except for keeping score—numbers—but it has two advantages: it is fun, and everyone can get involved.

Method

Set up a volleyball "court": maybe two chairs with some ribbon or rope between them to act as the net. Blow up a couple of balloons. Have a paper and pencil handy to keep score.

Divide the class into two teams and give each team a name. You can then start to play volleyball in the usual way, but you'll find the balloon moves much more slowly than a conventional volleyball. This gives students much more time to react and prepare themselves. It can sometimes be very comical how slowly the balloon moves in the air. Be careful of the sudden shock of a bursting balloon.

Bottle Spin

Level: Primary 1–4

Time taken: 10 minutes

Introduction

This is a means rather than an end—it is something that might well be placed in the scheme of a larger activity. However, this is not to say that it cannot be used on its own.

Method

All you need is a bottle—preferably rather heavy, such as an ordinary wine bottle. All children sit in a circle with the wine bottle lying down in the middle. Simply, spin the bottle firmly; when it stops, it will be pointing at one of the children. This child is given a point and is winning!

As an alternative to this basic method, you could make it a disadvantage for the bottle to be pointing at you (i.e., give them a forfeit).

If you ever have trouble finding a volunteer whilst teaching, this method is fair and respected: if the bottle points at you, it's your turn to empty the bin!

Brick-Stack Game

Level: Primary 1–6

Time taken: 10 minutes

Introduction

Skill and strategy are important in this fun game, and it can be made educational with the addition of questions to each brick. A set of wooden bricks can be bought or made.

Method

To play the simple game, stack the bricks into a tower. One by one, player by player, take one of the bricks from the stack and place it on top—easy at first, but more difficult as the game progresses.

The stack will wobble and appear ready to topple over, but, of course, it won't—until one unfortunate student picks the wrong brick or wobbles the stack so that the whole tower tumbles. Some children will try to distract their friends or try to wobble the table when it is their opponent's turn!

An educational alternative is to number the bricks and assign a question to each number. The student must answer the question correctly to win a point. The student (or team) with the most points wins; the student who topples the tower loses (could be both). You can have more than one set of questions, each tailored to your recent classroom topic. The first time I tried this method, I made the mistake of trying to write the questions on the bricks!

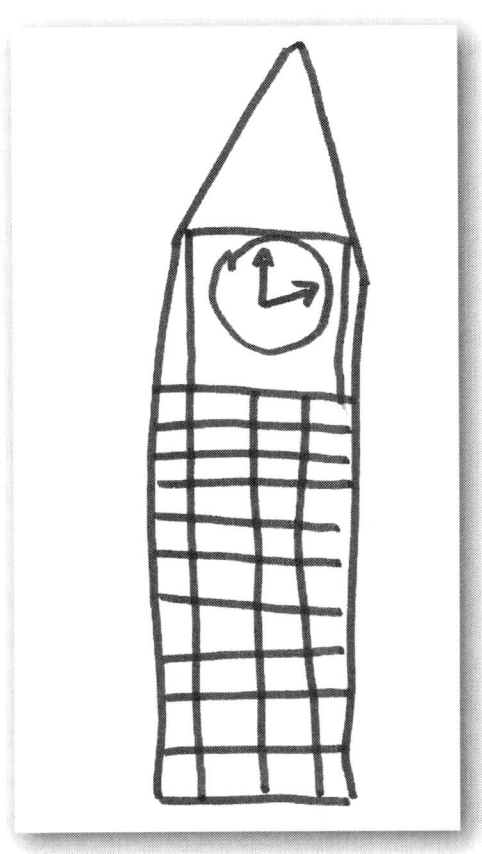

Barry Nicholson

Cardboard Rocket

Level: Primary 1–6

Time taken: 30-plus minutes

Introduction

Have you ever looked at the stars and wondered what it would be like to travel into space? How about designing and building your own rocket? This activity allows the imagination to run wild and ends in a full-sized class rocket!

Method

Design your rocket (or car, train, plane) first. Students can do this individually in their workbooks, or you can make it a class activity on the board. Together you can choose the best design—and it will be made into a full-sized rocket, maybe two or three meters in length.

You will need a large piece of cardboard—fridge packaging is ideal if you can find it, otherwise stick together smaller flattened cardboard boxes as required. Put the card flat on the floor. Draw the outline of the rocket on the card. The students' job is to colour the rocket, decorate it, and perhaps stick things to it (crepe paper, foil, sweet wrappings, etc.). You will end up with a beautiful class rocket. Perhaps make a stand for it or stick it on the wall. You may even use it as the basis for a role play.

Barry Nicholson

Colour Collecting

Level: Primary 3–6

Time taken: 15–20 minutes

Introduction

Colour is a fundamental in this world—we would be devoid of quality and texture without it. Recognition of colours and their English names is the aim here.

Method

Choose a colour; the children must then find objects that are this colour. There are a number of ways to arrange this. A first way is to arrange around your classroom or play area a number of things of your chosen colour. Upon your signal, the children try to find as many of these items as possible. Maybe the objects are very easy to see, making the children rush to collect them. A second way, after choosing a colour, is to ask the children to find objects over the space of, say, one week. Such objects can be placed on a class "colour table." This second method is far less competitive and provides a pleasant backdrop to your normal classes.

Crash

Level: Primary 1–4

Time taken: 10–15 minutes

Introduction

If you prefer potentially violent games, then this is the one for you. Tell your children to play gently so that noone gets hurt.

Method

Get the children to move around the room, preferably in a circle and in the same direction. When the teacher calls out an instruction to sit down, the children must do so—but they must do so in groups according to what is called. For example, "Sit down in threes" means they must rush to sit in groups of three. Any children left over can sit out, and the last ones left are the winners.

For variety incorporate your numbers into a story. Being the creative teacher that you are, this can be made up on the spot.

Barry Nicholson

Dressing-Up Race

Level: Primary 1–4

Time taken: 15 minutes

Introduction

Fashion! We seem preoccupied with it in this day and age, as a walk down any high street will demonstrate. But it is not just clothes themselves that capture the imagination, but also that magical thought of dressing up for a party or special occasion.

Method

You need to select a bundle of old clothes and, at best, two of each item (for your two teams). Don't use your best Sunday dinner jacket!

Each of your two teams elects one person to be "dressed up" first. At your signal, this person is dressed up by his teammates in floppy shirt, flowery hat, oversized shoes, and baggy trousers. All clothes must be worn in the correct places, and all buttons done up. The first team to dress their person correctly wins.

The flurry of team activity in this game is enough to confuse anybody, and an arm or a leg put in the wrong hole will not be uncommon. Your students must cooperate or be left in a muddle—and in second place.

Egyptian Mummy

Level: Primary 4–6

Time taken: 10 minutes

Introduction

Do you know the story of Tutankhamun? He was a fabulously rich king in Ancient Egypt, but he was only a boy. He died at a young age and was buried with all his treasure, mostly gold. Howard Carter discovered his tomb in the early twentieth century, but many people on his archaeological team died unexpected deaths. Was this the curse of Tutankhamun? Add this activity to a project on Ancient Egypt.

Method

Select one student to be the "mummy." You need a good supply of cheap toilet paper. The other students have to wrap the mummy from head to toe, except the face. Some parts of the body are easy to wrap (arms) whilst some are more difficult (the tummy). Have two teams compete against each other. Who can produce the best mummy? Don't forget to have your camera ready.

Barry Nicholson

Famous Person Quiz

Level: Primary 3–6

Time taken: 20 minutes

Introduction

Have you ever met a famous person? They come in all shapes and sizes, from football players to actors or pop stars or royalty. This game makes students guess the identity of a famous person using questions and is similar to Twenty Questions. I use it often as an icebreaker activity at the start of a course.

Method

First, you need to think up a list of famous people—some of whom are international stars and others well known in your locality. Write or type the names onto pieces of paper or cards. You may need to make a couple of sets as they tend to go missing.

To give the students the idea, you can go first. Pick one of the cards at random and announce, "I am this person. Who am I?" The students must then take turns, individually or in groups, asking one question about the person (Where are you from? What is your job? Are you a man or a woman? Are you a singer? etc.). A guess at a name counts as a question. The winning team is the first to correctly guess the name of the famous person. That team can then become the next person for the others to guess.

Extend this by having the groups make a poster about one of the people—put together, this can make a very creative wall display.

Fancy Dress Party

Level: Primary 1–6

Time taken: 20 minutes

Introduction

When we dress up, we become someone else, our identity is changed, and we are in disguise. Exploit this in a humorous way, allowing the children to be creative with whatever clothes they choose.

Method

You need to get a selection of old clothes, or clothes left over from a jumble sale. Make sure they are reasonably clean. Students can simply choose clothes and dress up in them but without the element of competition in a Dressing-Up Race. If resources are limited, select one child to be the dummy. Often the effect is hilarious, especially if you add a pair of dark glasses.

There are two variations: First, after dressing up, dance to music. Second, choose a theme from the start, such as "pirates" or "kings and queens," perhaps making the whole experience into a party with cakes and soda.

Feel Bags

Level: Primary 1–6

Time taken: 15–20 minutes

Introduction

A variation on those well-known blindfold games, without a blindfold. The sense of touch is just as important as the others, and the ability to feel and tell what something is without seeing it is both challenging and fun.

Method

Fill up a number of strong bags with various objects (according to your theme) for the children to feel and guess what they are. It is easy to tie this to a topic, such as classroom objects or fruit. According to the standard of your pupils, they can speak what they think it is, write it, or even draw it. Whoever guesses the most correctly is the winner (and gets to keep one of the objects).

A variation that I've tried a couple of times is to make this into a group competition. For this you need two bags of each, one for each team. Upon your word the first person in each team feels inside bag A. Once he or she has decided what the thing is, he or she must rush to the board to write or draw it. Carry on in similar fashion with bag B, bag C, and so on.

Barry Nicholson

Golden Bell

Level: Primary 3–6

Time taken: 20 minutes

Introduction

This activity is a quiz particularly suited to larger groups, and is a variation on a basic question-answer quiz. Before you start, see if you can get a small bell, preferably golden, for prominent display throughout the quiz. The winning team will get to ring the golden bell as their prize.

Method

Before you start, you need to prepare a list of twenty or so questions divided into three categories: easy (How do you spell teacher?), so-so (What is the capital of India?), and difficult (How many minutes are there in a day?).

Set the students up in groups of four or five. Give each group a small whiteboard and marker (or some sheets of plain paper as an alternative). Start with the easy questions. Make sure everyone can hear. As a group they come up with an answer and write it clearly on their whiteboard. When you give the prompt, the teams hold up their answers for you to see. If the answer is wrong, the team is out. If correct, the team stays for the next round. The last team remaining is the winner and gets to come to the front to collect its prize and "ring the golden bell."

Good, Horrid, In-Between

Level: Primary 1–4

Time taken: 10 minutes

Introduction

This is a good activity to elicit students' reactions to a number of things—to try and get some exaggerated expressions on their faces.

Method

Show pictures, books, or flashcards of anything you want (e.g., animals, food, or funny people) and try to elicit some expressive reactions, such as "ahhh!" or "hahaha!" or "mm, very nice!" and so on. Draw three lists on the board and write the things in the appropriate list according to the reactions. You might want to transform this into an "expressions competition," in which teams compete to pull the funniest faces when reacting to the things.

Barry Nicholson

Hunt the Thimble

Level: Primary 1–4

Time taken: 10–15 minutes

Introduction

This is a well-known party game with a sense of adventure. You must use your ingenuity and achieve the impossible—and make the game as hard as you can for your opponents.

Method

The organizer hides a thimble (or some small object) in a room or other defined area for the others to find within a certain time limit. The thimble must not be covered up by anything else (mostly), and the searchers have to be able to find the thimble without moving anything. This does not mean to say that you can't be crafty in where you hide the thimble, but remember not to make it too difficult or your children will despair!

Jeopardy Quiz

Level: Primary 3–6

Time taken: 30-plus minutes

Introduction

Rather than just one question to one team, one question to another, the Jeopardy Quiz copies the famous US quiz show and lets students choose their category and difficulty level from a gameboard. The quiz is good for review of recent class topics.

Method

You need to prepare a gameboard and a set of questions. On the board (or a large piece of paper) draw up a grid, say, five by five squares. Along the left, on the outside of the grid, write "100," "200," "300," "400," and "500" beside each of the rows. These are the points. Along the top write your five chosen categories above each of the columns. The categories could be recent class topics or a recent day trip or guest visitor to the school. Or you could just do it for fun!

Divide the class into teams of four or five. In turn, a team selects a category and score (e.g., "Famous People, two hundred points"). Ask the question; a correct answer in this case would get two hundred points. Throw the question open to the other groups if there is no answer or an incorrect answer.

Keep asking questions to the teams in turn until all the squares are taken or time is up. The winning team is the one with the highest score. Well done!

Letters Lucky Dip

Level: Primary 1–6

Time taken: 20 minutes

Introduction

The eyes of all primary children seem to light up at the mention of "ABC." For lower levels it is important to learn the alphabet in the first place, and for higher levels the alphabet—and in particular the letter sounds—can be presented and reviewed.

Method

The best way to do this activity is to have the following materials: magnetic letters, a whiteboard and pen, and a Lucky Dip bag. Sit the children in a semicircle around the whiteboard. In turn, a child takes a letter from the bag and sticks it to the board. Teach the phonic sound of the letter (e.g., the two main ways to pronounce "A" and so on). When one of the children thinks of a word that starts with that letter, he or she puts a hand up and tells you. If correct get the child to write it on the whiteboard and, if possible, draw a picture of the thing. Higher levels can write a complete sentence containing the word. Run through a few letters in this way, and review all letters and phonic sounds at the end.

I have played this activity time after time with the same class, and the class has never seemed to tire of it—perhaps because it combines fun with learning!

Letter Sort

Level: Primary 1–6

Time taken: 15 minutes

Introduction

This is definitely a participation activity that creative, conservative children will enjoy. Don't seriously try this activity if your class is rowdy or ill-behaved!

Method

Each child is assigned to be a common letter. The letter is written on a big piece of paper that is then attached to his or her front. The children move around and make as many words as possible with themselves. You could control this activity yourself or just leave the children to their own devices. If a word is made, you can write it on a list on the board.

Barry Nicholson

Measurement-Parts of the Body

❖ ❖ ❖

Level: Primary 1–6

Time taken: 20 minutes

Introduction

Children come in all shapes and sizes, something that can be capitalized upon with this activity; we are all different! This lesson on body measurements can be nicely tied into the topic of comparatives and superlatives.

Method

The method is simple. Divide your class into three or four groups of four. Each group needs a ruler, and members of the group will work together to measure parts of the body. Such parts might be the head, neck, arm, tummy, leg, foot, and so on. Pupils record the length of each part, which can be compared in a final session. You might like to record all measurements on a class chart in order to compare them.

The children will learn about their physical differences, but just as importantly, they will realize that to do some jobs, they must cooperate and help each other.

Measurement-Height Line-Up

Level: Primary 1–6

Time taken: 15–20 minutes

Introduction

The activity also shows differences, this time in height. Again, this activity is essentially tied to comparatives and superlatives. You will have to exercise control and order in this activity.

Method

Line the children up, in any order, but then start sorting them according to height. Shorter students go to one end, taller to the other. They will probably get the hang of this quickly, with only some "fine-tuning" provided by you.

You can then drill questions and answers.

Who is the tallest?—Thomas is the tallest.

Who is the shortest?—Simon is the shortest.

A straightforward adjustment is to place a chair at the end of the line near the tallest child and get a shorter child to stand on the chair and then ask the following:

Who is the tallest?—Betty is the tallest.

Then place a table next to this with another of the shorter children standing on top; similarly, make "short" people at the other end by getting tall children to sit down on a chair or on the floor. The short students enjoy being tall, and the tall students enjoy being short.

Mingle Survey-Questionnaire

Level: Primary 5–6

Time taken: 15–20 minutes

Introduction

The exchange of information is important, especially if this information is useful or interesting to the other party. The lack of information that needs to be shared is the "information gap"; only by practicing their English skills can the students share information and fill this "gap."

Method

The activity can be adapted to many topics. Draw up a questionnaire in chart form with questions down the side and "Student 1," "Student 2," "Student 3," and so on along the top. Run through the questions as a class first to check understanding. Then comes the surprising order to stand up, walk around, and ask each other the set of questions, marking down the answers as they go.

When all students have had a go at asking the questions, it is time to pool the information. Get each student to tell the class one thing about one of the people he or she asked. Maybe you could write this on a class chart on the board (or on a handout of your own to be copied and given out later).

A good topic for a Mingle Survey—Questionnaire is personal details: "Where do you live?" "How old are you?" and so on.

Murals

Level: Primary 1–6

Time taken: 20 minutes

Introduction

Creativity is fun! So often these days this skill is submerged within a sea of science or facts, but creativity, for example a large mural, adds colour and life to the classroom routine.

Method

There are two ways to make a class mural. The first is to get a large piece of art paper, gather your pupils around it, and ask them to draw things connected to your topic. The problem with this, apart from the lack of elbow space, is that some of the drawings will be upsidedown! Despite this, a colourful effect is usually achieved—such as an animal mural.

The second way to make a mural is to draw a picture separately, cut it out and then stick it onto the large paper. With this, pupils can work more on their own and be more individually creative. Also, the cut pictures can be arranged by you in a more effective manner. Beforehand you could draw some simple background on the large paper (such as trees) to ensure the mural is the right way up.

Pass the Parcel

Level: Primary 1–4

Time taken: 15 minutes

Introduction

This is a classic party activity, but it's also well used in the primary school. It takes a bit more preparation and has no guarantee of success in an unruly class. However, explained and managed well, it is fun and can be as creative as you wish.

Method

Decide which small object will be the prize; it is easy to find something related to your topic or current class project. Wrap the thing up in successive layers of paper, either using sticky tape or string to secure each layer. A forfeit is put in with each layer.

Students sit in a circle. Start up some music. The parcel is passed around the circle until the music is stopped. When this is done, that student takes one layer off the parcel and has to take the forfeit (singing in front of the others is a good one). Then the parcel continues, layer after layer, student after student, forfeit after forfeit. At last, one lucky child gets the prize!

Percussion Band

Level: Primary 1–4

Time taken: 15–20 minutes

Introduction

Music is a universal language that can be put to good use in the classroom. A few classic activities feature music, but it is also worth singling out music on its own. The children themselves can "create" music, albeit a little ragged round the edges.

Method

After having introduced the subject of music, present to the children a few simple methods of making "music": beating on a pot or pan, blowing across the top of a bottle, rubbing two rough sticks together, and so on. Demonstrate the methods first and then elect a student or two to play each.

The best way to proceed is to start a clear, basic beat and get the children to join in one at a time. Another way is to play some music or a popular song and allow them to join in. Tape the end result if you like. Whatever method you use, this activity is great fun, but don't forget your headache tablets!

Pin the Tail on the Dinosaur

Level: Primary 1–4

Time taken: 10–15 minutes

Introduction

We all know that it should be Pin the Tail on the Donkey, but somehow a dinosaur conjures up more imagery. This popular blindfold game is fun and enjoyable, even if rather limited in scope.

Method

Either draw or get the pupils to draw a large dinosaur on a piece of art paper or on the board. There should be one thing missing from the paper—a tail!

One by one, children are blindfolded, turned around three times, and asked to pin on the tail. Usually the children will be quite dizzy and pin the tail in a peculiar place. Other children will be strangely accurate.

If you feel creative, you can adapt this game into whatever you want: Pin the Eyes on the Monkey.

Pronunciation Mingle

Level: Primary 4–6

Time taken: 10 minutes

Introduction

Pronunciation is a common hurdle for all nonnative speakers, and it is, of course, important to be able to distinguish some sounds, such as the classic *Ship or Sheep?* lesson.

Method

Write sentences or short phrases on cards; these sentences are best based around a common sound, such as "the man with the fan is sitting in the van," "six sticks," "wet, windy Wednesday," and so on. Students mingle and practice these with each other; after saying the sentence or phrase, they swap cards and continue to another classmate.

As an additional activity to this, you can get your students to write a short passage using many examples of one sound. This can be read out to the whole class or be made into a simple tongue twister.

Raise Your Left Leg...

Level: Primary 1–6

Time taken: 15 minutes

Introduction

There is frequently great confusion between "left" and "right," especially amongst younger children (but sometimes, surprisingly, with older students). You can introduce or review left and right with this activity, but you may at times have to be patient—and the children might delight in deliberately getting things wrong.

Method

Make a pair of cards for each child, one with "left" written on it the other with "right." Clearly give each child the "left" card in the left hand and the "right" card in the right hand—easier said than done.

Call out instructions, slowly and clearly, such as, "Left arm!" Hopefully, the children should all raise their left arm. Go around and Correct those who've got it wrong. Maybe point at the student and laughingly say no.

After having run through a few left arms and right arms to your satisfaction, try "right leg" and "left leg." You can go a long way in terms of difficulty—as far as "right arm and left leg" closely followed by "left arm and right leg." The world is your oyster in this fun activity!

Role Plays

Level: Primary 3–4

Time taken: 20 minutes

Introduction

Communicative skills come to the fore with a role play. If properly set up, a role play is useful in many situations and is both productive and creative.

Method

I will consider the method for two prime examples of classroom role-play: shopping and the restaurant.

Shopping is universally enjoyed and, as a subject, can be tied to things such as food, money, or requests. Here, in its basic form, it is an aid to communication and learning related vocabulary.

Set up a table at the front of the class and arrange several everyday shopping items on it. Select a confident child to be the shopkeeper. The other students stand in a line and wait their turn to "buy" something. They can use simple language, such as, "How much is this?" or something more complicated (e.g., haggle over the price). Enhance the role play by using fake money or a traditional-style shopping basket.

For the restaurant role play, students sit around a "dinner table" with one student as the waiter. Here they can practice some previously drilled sentences, such as, "Can I have the menu, please?" or "I would like…" Use props again: tablecloth, knives and forks, plastic food, and the like.

Scavenger Hunt

Level: Primary 3–6

Time taken: 15-plus minutes

Introduction

Searching for things is somehow fascinating, and your students will delight in searching for some of the wonderful things you ask them to find.

Method

This is similar to colour collecting except that you're looking for objects from a list rather than colours. Make up a list of weird and wonderful objects for your students to attempt to find, such as the following:

- An insect
- A pair of glasses
- A foreign coin

Give them a time limit to find the objects—possibly on a day trip or overnight—and see how many each team can find. It is obvious that this activity must be adapted for younger children who perhaps could search for things in the classroom or within the school.

Seeds and Plants

Level: Primary 1–6

Time taken: 20 minutes

Introduction

Natural life of all varieties is fascinating to children. Things we may take for granted, such as seeds growing, create excitement and enjoyment for children. This activity allows them to see nature in action, and allows for observations well after the lesson itself.

Method

You are about to plant some seeds! Choose some fruit with seeds inside (like lemons or oranges). Gather your pupils around a large preparation area and show them that you have the fruit. Cut up the fruit and count the seeds as you find them—make sure there is enough for each student to get a seed. Give each pupil the following:

- A small container (plastic cup)
- Some small stones
- Some earth
- A seed
- A plastic bag (to put over the top)

How you do this is up to you, but the better the class, the less teacher control. Once they have everything, they can plant their seed. Make it clear that the seed needs sunlight and water to grow.

With a little luck, your students should come back to you in a few weeks' time with a seedling to show.

Shout Out!

Level: Primary 1–6

Time taken: 10 minutes

Introduction

Participation is a major key throughout this book, sometimes taking a complex form and sometimes simple. Here, participation is as simple as can be. The activity ties well into a pronunciation practice session.

Method

Assuming one is practicing some point of pronunciation, for example "O" as in "hot," the following method is used. Make up a story that has examples of "O" words (body, sock, clock, etc.) and read it to your students. Explain that every time they hear the "O" sound, they must shout out, "Now!" See if your students can correctly identify all the sounds, and help them if they do not notice a sound. Possibly divide the class into two teams to make a competition.

Of course, you don't have to use pronunciation sounds—you could use animals, names, or any subject at all. Participation in the form of shouting out is lively, simple, and effective.

Sink or Float?

❖ ❖ ❖

Level: Primary 1–4

Time taken: 10–15 minutes

Introduction

This is an activity that contrasts two opposites in a very straightforward way. It is a scientific test—one that involves guesswork and one that children will enjoy.

Method

Fill either a bucket or the class sink with water, about two-thirds full. Make this area as visible as possible to the whole class. Collect a number of objects, some that float and some that do not. Place an object into the water to see if it sinks or floats. It is a good idea to have a guess at whether the object will float or not—possibly even a class vote.

With some things it is easy to tell if they will sink or float, others difficult. Some objects might be the following:

- An egg
- An orange
- Chalk
- Cheese
- Chocolate

As the objects go into the water, make a note of the results—this gives the activity a more scientific slant.

Simple Exercises

Level: Primary 1–6

Time taken: 10–15 minutes

Introduction

Being able to follow instructions related to physical movement is tested here, but also the activity highlights the importance of physical exercises—however simple—for a healthy lifestyle.

Method

At best go out to the playground where you can all stand in a circle, a little apart from each other. Start to run through some simple exercises as a group, such as the following:

- Stretching up
- Touching your toes
- Twirling around
- Jumping
- Skipping

After running through these as a group, run through them again taking turns. You will probably have to demonstrate.

Although the students will probably speak no English during this activity, they must listen and understand your simple instructions.

Skittles

Level: Primary 1–4

Time taken: 15 minutes

Introduction

This is a popular game, and one that most children will know already. It combines coordination skills with a fun, preferably outdoor, game.

Method

A plastic skittles set can be bought quite cheaply, or use empty plastic bottles and a tennis ball. Line up the skittles, or put them in a nine- or ten-pin setup. Either individually or in two teams, pupils attempt to knock over as many skittles as possible. Count the number of "hits" to see who wins.

In terms of variations, one way is to assign each skittle a number based on some sort of points system. As an alternative, you might like to know that I'm trying to think of an activity where people are the skittles: an interesting idea that might stop those who are waiting their turn from getting bored!

Stage Plays

Level: Primary 4–6

Time taken: 30-plus minutes

Introduction

Children love to act; it is a combination of speech, action, voice, tone, and emotion. Fairy tales can be acted out successfully. Girls love to be Cinderella or a princess. Boys might enjoy being a superhero. Here I suggest using the story of the *Titanic* as it is very visual and involves a number of characters and props.

Method

Familiarize your students with the story of the *Titanic* first. You can do this through a story book, clips from a documentary, or your own pictures. Make up some characters that your students will act out later. Don't forget to ask students questions about the story and characters to make sure they understand it.

You can divide the class into small groups and have each group write its own script, or you could try to write the script on the board following suggestions by the children. It might be an idea to make copies for the students if you have this facility. Then comes the fun part—acting the scripts out. You might keep it simple, or you could go to town with props, clothes, music, and the like.

The *Titanic* can be tied in with many classroom topics: pirates, transportation, music (the band played as the *Titanic* sank), world records, and so on.

Target Practice (Bucket Throw)

Level: Primary 1–4

Time taken: 15 minutes

Introduction

This is a game in particular for lower levels and, whilst simple, is a lot of fun. Physical coordination and teamwork are the main things to be tested.

Method

Use a large classroom or playground area. Set up a number of buckets or similar containers, some forward and some farther back. Give each bucket a point score according to its difficulty level. Either working by themselves or in two teams, pupils see how many points they can score by throwing a beanbag or ball into the bucket.

The school where I worked before had a large-scale open day where it was necessary to devise a game suitable for large numbers of children—and the bucket throw was it! Not only was it very easy to set up, but it could also be used time and time again, "heavy duty" so to speak, for the duration of the day.

Time Acting

Level: Primary 1–6

Time taken: 15–20 minutes

Introduction

One of the more complicated aspects of learning English is that of telling the time. The use of the words "to" and "past" in telling time tend to confuse learners of all ages! But once your children are initially drilled, there is an alternative exercise for reviewing times apart from the traditional clockface print stamp: time acting.

Method

Write some simple times on some cards, to be placed facedown on the table or in a Lucky Dip bag. Students will feel happier doing this activity as a group, so get two or three of them up at a time. They select a "timecard," and this is the time they must act out to the rest of the class. They do this by moving their arms and legs until they look like a clock showing the time—at first they won't know which leg to put where. You can reinforce the correct answer by drawing it on the board or displaying it on a toy clockface.

Time and Big Ben

Level: Primary 1–6

Time taken: 15 minutes

Introduction

One approach to learning how to tell the time was outlined in Time Acting. Here is a different approach that involves making a model clock tower—in this case a 3-D Big Ben.

Method

Depending on how brave you feel, you can approach this in two ways. The first way is to have each student make his or her own clock tower from paper or a thin card. Fold the paper in half then in half again (lengthways) so that it is divided into four equal parts. These are the four walls of the tower. Students can put a clock on each face; a door; windows; and maybe some trees, flowers, and people. Then, with your help, they can stick the tower together using tape or glue. What's the time?

The second method is more ambitious, and it is to create a large metre or two-metre-high clock tower using cardboard (the large kind of cardboard they use to pack fridges in). Follow the same procedure, but on a much larger scale. You will have a lot more decorating to do; and you can cut some windows and a door if you like. Try attaching a toy or real clock to one of the faces, and you might have a go at making a chime, just like the real Big Ben.

Tongue Twisters

Level: Primary 3–6

Time taken: 10-plus minutes

Introduction

Reading rather troublesome words rapidly is the name of the game in a wicked test of pronunciation. You can practice a mispronounced letter or just have some fun with this activity.

Method

Many different tongue twisters exist, a few of the more common being the following:

- She sells seashells on the seashore.
- Round the rugged rocks, the ragged rascal ran.
- Red lorry, yellow lorry.

You can set the activity up in a number of ways, but the best way is to demonstrate the tongue twister first, get the class to repeat it, and then get individuals to repeat it. You will get rounds of laughter from the students laughing at each other's attempts—until it's their turn. The whole activity could be turned into a pronunciation competition, or you could put the tongue twisters into a Lucky Dip bag, or you could use them in a Pronunciation Mingle.

Twenty Questions

Level: Primary 3–6

Time taken: 10-plus minutes

Introduction

Guessing games are always fun and often have an element of frustration, sifting through the clues for the answer. Challenge the children in this way with a game of Twenty Questions.

Method

One person chooses a well-known character who the others have to guess by asking questions. The person answering can only respond with a yes or no, and those guessing only have twenty attempts at finding out who the person is (hence, "Twenty" Questions). They could ask questions about where a person is from, what his or her job is, and so on. A guess counts as a question. In a similar way, if nineteen questions have not produced a result, then it stands to reason that the twentieth question must be a guess at who the person is.

This activity is popular as you need no props to play it, and it can be played with any number of players from two upwards.

Twister

Level: Primary 1–4

Time taken: 15 minutes

Introduction

Thinking is combined with physical coordination here. Although the game is commercially available, you can just as easily make your own version. The commercially available set uses colours—but you could be more creative and use any set of words you wish!

Method

You need a very large base paper, in total about one and a half by one and a half metres, divided into a grid of four-by-four squares. Stick cardboard together to make this base, or alternatively chalk the grid onto the ground. Each row of squares on the grid has a particular colour (or whatever).

You need to either make a spinner or a Lucky Dip bag, where options are something like "right foot blue" or "left arm red." The more time you have, the more professional the finished setup will be.

To play, spin the spinner or draw from the Lucky Dip bag to find a card. Each of the three or four children playing moves to the position as told by the spinner or the Lucky Dip card ("Put your left leg on yellow," etc.). As you progress with more instructions, it gets increasingly difficult for the children not to fall over—those who do are out.

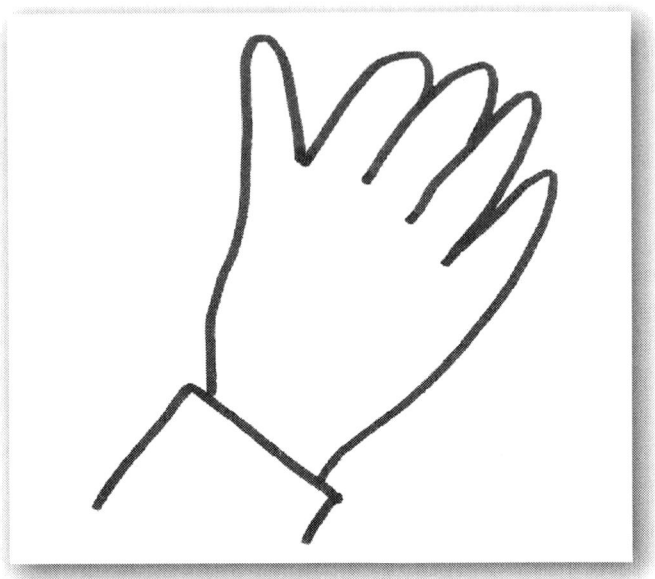

Word Associations

Level: Primary 5–6

Time taken: 10 minutes

Introduction

Lots of words are connected together, and many words mean the same thing. This activity plays on such links and provides you with a verbal dictionary of associations.

Method

Work out some order for the students to respond—probably sitting in a circle. Start off with a simple word (e.g., cat). The next student must say a word associated with this, like dog. This goes on from student to student in a never-ending chain:

…bone…skeleton…pirate…ship…sea…swimming…

Part 4
Paper Activities

Activities involving paper are perhaps more conventional but just as much fun. Paper is a fundamental academic tool, and good use of it leads to good education. Even though it is being superseded in many ways by information technology, notably computers, its role in primary teaching remains paramount.

Having said this, a good many of the following games can be played using a computer drawing programme—if you are fortunate enough to have this facility!

ABC Words

Level: Primary 1–6

Time taken: 15 minutes

Introduction

If you wish to take a rest for a few moments, this activity serves the purpose well. It is similar to A Word Beginning With and, likewise, tests vocabulary skills.

Method

Divide your class into groups of three or four. Each group has a list of the letters of the alphabet and must try to think of one word that starts with each letter. Some letters (like A, B, or C) will be easy; others (like X, Y, or Z) are more problematic. Encourage your students to be inventive, trying to find a long or unusual word with the aid of a dictionary. Even give a prize for the best word.

Anagrams

Level: Primary 1–6

Time taken: 10-plus minutes

Introduction

Similar to the game Constantinople, the main thrust of this activity is to rearrange letters from words. It also has an extra creative element—the ability to form new, often weird, words of your own.

Method

You need to find a vocabulary set related to the class topic and spend some time rearranging the letters in these words into strange new words. Your students have to decode the words back into their original forms. For example, if the topic is fruit and vegetables, they might decode the following:

- seppal (apples)
- nanabas (bananas)
- trocar (carrot)
- buccmure (cucumber)

You could incorporate the anagrams into a story; or all the words in the story could be anagrams—though you'll have to put in the necessary preparation time.

A Word Beginning With...

Level: Primary 3–6

Time taken: 10–15 minutes

Introduction

Good for teamwork and imagination, this activity is refreshingly popular and allows the teacher to take a break.

Method

Divide the children into teams of three or four, and one member of each group is the scribe. Choose a letter from the alphabet and see how many words the children can find that start with that letter. It is best to set a time limit for this. Obviously, the team with the most correct words wins.

As an extra task, you can get the students to write sentences with the words.

Barry Nicholson

Blindfold Drawing

Level: Primary 1–6

Time taken: 15 minutes

Introduction

There is something peculiar about closing your eyes in the knowledge that someone else is around. What will the person do? Poke you in the ribs or make fun of you? I hope, instead, he or she helps you with Blindfold Drawing, which proves that even the best of us can get things strangely wrong.

Method

The method is simple—whilst blindfolded, the child is instructed to draw something that you know the child can easily draw (a house, a cat, a person…). Getting the right things in the right place is quite a challenge. It is most rewarding to see the reactions of the other children who can see the strange picture taking shape. The blindfolded child makes false corrections in an effort to eliminate what he or she perceives as an error! Just as rewarding is the finished picture and the drawer's reaction to it.

With a good class, you can play this game forever.

Body Construction

Level: Primary 1–4

Time taken: 15 minutes

Introduction

This is an activity that works best with small groups or one-to-one teaching. A child must actively think and create "people" in an imaginative way.

Method

Use clear instructions and have patience here. Each child has a piece of A4 paper divided into four parts. Each child draws a funny head on the top part of his or her paper then folds the top part of the paper over so just the neck can be seen. Then all papers are passed around to the next student, who draws a funny body. He or she also folds over the paper, this time so that only the waist is showing. The paper is passed on again and the legs are drawn, and then again for the feet.

When the body is complete, the folded papers can be opened up to reveal a strange alien—and bursts of laughter!

Collages

Level: Primary 1–4

Time taken: 20 minutes

Introduction

Sometimes a classroom wall needs to be brightened up, and a good way to do this is to use collages—a combination of students' pictures stuck onto one big piece of paper.

Method

You will need a large piece of coloured paper and some smaller A4 pieces for each student. Give the small papers to the students and get them to draw pictures according to your theme. Common themes are animals, weather symbols, shops, and buildings in the city.

Help the children cut out their drawings, and encourage them to stick their artwork onto the big paper. You can help them position their work on the paper so that it is more decorative. Try stringing together a whole series of collages along the classroom or corridor wall for a fully enjoyable visual display.

Constantinople

Level: Primary 3–6

Time taken: 10-plus minutes

Introduction

Reviewing "ABC" is not only for the very young, and the realization that letters can be rearranged to make completely different words is basic in the learning of English.

Method

So this is also a letter rearrangement activity. Choose a long word (such as Constantinople—hence the name) and write it clearly on the board. The idea is to form as many new words as possible from the letters in your long word. You can only use a letter once, and you cannot include words of less than three characters. Thus from "Constantinople" you can make over twenty words, like the following:

- Constant
- Plastic
- Pole
- Tin
- Lost
- Static

Creative Badges

Level: Primary 1–6

Time taken: 10 minutes

Introduction

In the first lesson, you may have made name badges. Now it's time to be a little more creative and make decorative badges representing your chosen theme.

Method

Your theme could be animals (butterfly badges work well), parts of the body (a bone or heart), or a star or medal shape. You need to copy enough to go around the class, and some children will demand more than one copy.

Encourage the students to decorate their badges well and cut them out neatly. They can be attached to the student with sticky tape or a clothes peg. The students love showing off their badges to each other. Make sure you have a mirror handy, too.

Crosswords

Level Primary 3–6

Time taken: 10–15 minutes

Introduction

Everyone knows this world famous pastime, but how many teachers have adapted it to the classroom? Although the crossword from *The Times* is out of the question, easier versions fill the gaps in your lesson plan.

Method

You can draw crosswords in a number of styles, from the "box and black out" crossword (*The Times*) to a "skeleton" crossword that just shows the boxes where letters actually exist. The latter is better for our purposes.

When constructing a crossword, begin with a long word in the middle as this will give you a better starting point to connect on other words. Chop and change your skeleton grid a number of times before you get a final version.

For the clues the most common method is to draw a picture (see "Picture Gap-Fills"), although an anagram or cryptic clue work well with higher levels. Don't forget that the children can construct crosswords of their own, too!

Describe and Draw

Level: Primary 1–6

Time taken: 10–15 minutes

Introduction

This is another activity that can fit into a good many topics. It is both fun and practical, testing listening and pronunciation skills aswell as descriptive and imaginative skills.

Method

According to the topic at hand, describe a picture to a class or individual child. Then ask the class or child to draw what you described. Topics that work well follow:

- Animals
- Physical descriptions
- Monsters or dinosaurs

Make sure that when you describe the thing, you start with a larger or more central part of the picture first. You can come up with the strangest things!

The most enjoyable part is to show everyone each other's pictures—perhaps revealing them one by one to increase tension.

Dot-to-Dot

Level: Primary 1–3

Time taken: 10 minutes

Introduction

This is another classic paper activity, and like a few others, it's produced in great quantity in classroom publications. However, have you ever been creative enough to produce a dot-to-dot of your own?

Method

The key to producing your own dot-to-dot is to keep it simple; too complicated, and you'll get confused drawing it, and they'll get confused joining it! Give yourself a test run by drawing something simple, such as a tree. You will soon learn to draw all the dots first (visualizing the picture as you go) and then write the numbers afterwards. Any child will jump to complete and colour your finished article.

Journal Writing

Level: Primary 1–6

Time taken: 10-plus minutes

Introduction

If the students are staying overnight at their school or camp, then it is a good idea to have them write a journal. It is an introspective activity but allows the child to reflect on the day, and it provides a permanent record of their camp.

Method

You can preproduce a journal booklet (perhaps A4 size) with a cover sheet and lined pages, one day for each, with the day and date at the top. Alternatively, just use a small notebook.

Encourage the students to write more than just a description of the day. How did they feel? What did they expect? What do they think tomorrow will be like? It might be a good idea to write questions or prompts for each day for the students to answer and respond to. For example, if they watched a film clip that day, how did they feel when they watched it? Who were the main characters? Did they enjoy the film? In this way you can prompt information from the students that they can write in their journal.

Some children may write personal things in their journal, and you should be careful not to invade their privacy. But if they are up to it, you can try getting some of them to read their journal aloud.

Making Books

Level: Primary 1–6

Time taken: 20 minutes

Introduction

Books come in all shapes and sizes and have all sorts of purposes. Children should learn at an early age that books are a very useful tool, and they can be used to our advantage in a very effective way.

Method

Each child can make a book of his or her own. It is best to demonstrate the method first before the children attempt it.

Give each child two or three pieces of A4 paper, each folded in half and inserted inside each other to make the basic book shape. The pages can be stapled or stuck together. The front page is the first (and most important) to decorate—the child's name and book title should be clearly written. Each page that follows will be divided into two parts: the top part for a colourful picture and the bottom part for writing. The writing gives some information about the picture and should be written clearly and neatly.

Of course, it is up to you to choose a topic, but making a book is a convenient way to review a recent class project.

Practical English Summercamp Activities

Matching Exercise

Level: Primary 1–6

Time taken: 10–15 minutes

Introduction

The ability to group things according to a common denominator is basic; to classify and group are the first stages of analysis. When thinking if two stimuli go together or not, you are actively checking to see if things belong to the same set.

Method

The most straightforward way to use matching is to write a list of words or phrases on one side of a piece of paper and another list of words or phrases on the other. The words on one side match those on the other, which, of course, are out of order. Students must either draw a line from word to matching word or copy out the two parts on a separate sheet. You could easily combine this with a Sentence Construction exercise.

Another matching method is to put all the words on cards, with the first half of the word or phrase on some cards and the second half on the others. Students take turns picking a card from each side and hopefully find a match (this is very similar to Pelmanism).

Lower levels can match pictures with words; higher levels can match questions with answers or problems with solutions.

Paper Football Pitch

Level: Primary 1–6

Time taken: 20 minutes

Introduction

Most children like football and will eagerly tell you their favourite team and players. You can bring football into the classroom without breaking anything with this paper-based activity.

Method

To make a football pitch, you'll need a large piece of green paper. One of the children can mark the centre line, goal, penalty lines, and corners. All of the children can draw and cut out players to be stuck onto the pitch. Leave a small tab on the base of the players' feet so that you can stick the tab to the paper and have the players "stand up." Goals can be made to "stand up" in a similar way, making your paper-football pitch 3-D rather than a 2-D collage. You might even try a game of football on it.

Paper Puzzle

Level: Primary 1–4

Time taken: 15 minutes

Introduction

Destruction-reconstruction is the name of the game here, but make sure your pupils know the meaning of "puzzle" by showing them a real puzzle or one of your own.

Method

Give the children an A4 or A3 sheet of paper and instruct them to draw a large, colourful picture on it. When it's completed, the children can cut their picture into about eight or ten pieces. Stop all those in their path who snip, snip, snip little pieces as small as fingernail clippings! Also, don't force a child to cut up his or her picture if he or she feels it is good enough as it is—though you should have already primed the children that their treasured artwork is in for the chop.

Once "destruction" is complete, the children can try out each other's puzzles and test them for difficulty. Thus the puzzle is an amusing activity in itself.

Pelmanism

Level: Primary 1–6

Time taken: 10 minutes

Introduction

Matching and grouping skills can be combined with fun and thinking in this "traditional" practical activity. And children never seem to tire of it!

Method

The method is similar to that of the Matching Exercise. This time all the cards to be matched are put on a table together (instead of in two groups). Students take turns turning over two cards, and if the cards match (pictures, words, questions and answers, etc.), he or she wins a point.

After a few turns, your students will start to remember the location of some of the cards, making selection easier.

I played this game once on a glass-topped table, which let me observe entertaining methods of cheating!

Picture Description

Level: Primary 5–6

Time taken: 15-plus minutes

Introduction

Description goes hand in hand with creativity. You cannot only see exactly what you see, you can also see behind a picture, make things up about it, "read between the lines." As if to show the need for even basic description skills, a colleague recently commented that when his students were asked to describe a picture of his living room, they readily noted a large TV and sofa but did not mention that the room had four walls, a ceiling, and a floor.

Method

Choose any picture you like—but ones with less to see are often more difficult. With lower levels you will be asking for pure description; with higher levels you will be wanting some "hidden" information. For pure description ask your students to look for the following:

- Situation (place, time of day, weather…)
- People (expressions, physical description…)
- What is going on (playing a sport, shopping…)

Reading "behind the picture" might reveal the following:

- What has happened before or what will happen
- What sort of personality the people have
- The making up of a story based on the picture
- If the student has had an experience like it

Picture Gap-Fill

Level: Primary 1–6

Time taken: 10–15 minutes

Introduction

Why not combine vocabulary with the visual? This is an often neglected but very useful paper activity—one that you can easily have a go at making yourself.

Method

You need to write a simple story suited to the level of your students, and preferably one that uses a lot of visual imagery (try *The House that Jack Built* or *Cinderella*). Write the story clearly on a piece of paper but leave out some of the visual words, replacing them with a picture followed by a gap. The students, realizing what the picture is, fill the missing word in the gap.

Quite extensive stories can be written like this, or the whole thing can be made more cryptic by drawing something a bit more obscure. Get the children to write stories of their own, for each other to "translate."

Poem Construction

Level: Primary 4–6

Time taken: 15-plus minutes

Introduction

Adjective poems! Three cheers for imagination! Poetry is an excellent way to give children a chance to express their creative powers, even if they need to be over-enthusiastically prompted. Adjective poems are simple to complete as a stimulus is already given and begs some further description.

Method

Decide on a topic (seasons, members of the family, methods of transport, etc.) and draw up a handout in which the students must fill in the blanks. For example, if the topic is seasons, write the following:

- Spring is _____
- Summer is _____
- Autumn is _____
- Winter is _____

As the child works down the list, his or her choice of words becomes more difficult—but more creative. I have had examples such as "Summer is ice-cream joy" or "Winter is a sad song."

Ask the children to read their poems aloud—this presentation stage, if done well, should be the best part of the activity.

Sentence Construction

Level: Primary 4–6

Time taken: 10-plus minutes

Introduction

Most parents worry that their child is not learning "fluent" English. Taking single words and forming context (a sentence) is increasingly seen as one important element in a child's grasp of "fluency."

Method

For sentence construction, you can either give your students a single word, around which a sentence must be made, or a series of words, which must be combined into a sentence. Examples follow:

frog
"The frog jumped into the river."

frog / trees / England
"The frog jumped into the river by the trees in England."

frog / jump over / look at
"A green frog jumped over the log to look at the moon."

In similar style comes paragraph construction—a little more difficult. You might, for example, have to direct the students' writing (example 1), though this is not always so structured (example 2).

1. station / train arrives early / many people / Mr. Jones late / he misses train
2. First sentence includes "station."
   Second sentence includes "arrive."
   Third sentence includes "Mr. Jones."

Snap!

Level: Primary 1–4

Time taken: 10 minutes

Introduction

Recognition of two similar or identical things is an important skill, especially amongst younger children. Snap! is a good way to test this skill.

Method

You will need to buy or make some cards that contain pairs of pictures identical to each other.

Stand your pupils around a central table and place all cards in one pile in front of you. Turn over two cards simultaneously, and if they match, your students shout out "Snap!" The first to shout is the winner.

Not only are pictures good for this game but also words or matching sentences (see "Matching Exercise").

Sound Snap!

Level: Primary 3–6

Time taken: 10 minutes

Introduction

Sound Snap! is much the same as Snap! except that it matches sounds instead of visuals. It is related to the ever-important topic of phonics and correct pronunciation.

Method

The method is the same as is for Snap! but important here is how Sound Snap! is an excellent activity for teaching vowel phonics. This time, students try to match words with the same vowel sounds (e.g., cat matches bat, or house matches mouse). The matching of vowels is related to rhyming and poetry (see "Poem Construction").

Spot the Difference

Level: Primary 1–4

Time taken: 10–15 minutes

Introduction

Spot The Difference essentially involves the comparison of two things and can fit into a lesson on comparatives and superlatives.

Method

You need to find two pictures or objects to compare. Sometimes the differences are obvious (e.g., summer and winter) and sometimes less obvious (e.g., the number of hairs on a man's head). Of course, there is also the traditional puzzle book *Spot The Difference*, which compares two cartoon pictures. Whichever way, note down as many differences as you can, and see who comes up with the most.

Stories from Words

Level: Primary 3–6

Time taken: 15-plus minutes

Introduction

Just like sentence or paragraph construction, this takes a number of elements that must be combined into some coherent whole.

Method

The "elements" of this activity are whatever words you care to choose—maybe a group of words related to each other, connected with a class project, or even chosen at random from a dictionary. These six or seven words must somehow feature in the student's story. Stress to your children that the words must fit in as naturally as possible, and that the words must be spaced within the story—for example, a maximum of one word per paragraph. It will be refreshing to learn that your students do have imagination after all!

Barry Nicholson

Treasure Chest and Money

Level: Primary 1–4

Time taken: 20 minutes

Introduction

Money may be the root of all evil, but it can also be a source of pleasure—especially if it is toy money. Combined with gold coins, diamonds, crystal necklaces, and rubies, you can make a treasure chest.

Method

Photocopy some toy money (real money if you dare), and find pictures of diamonds and necklaces to copy, too. Glossy magazines and Sunday supplements are a good source.

Make sure there are plenty of copies for all the children as money disappears fast. Some students will want to keep the "treasure" for themselves, but it is very effective to make a collage or decorate a cardboard box to make a 3-D treasure chest. Students can simply stick their treasure and jewellery onto the treasure chest.

Word Chart

Level: Primary 1–6

Time taken: 15-plus minutes

Introduction

Similar to a Vocabulary Dictionary, this compiles new words together, this time as a class effort. It can be a colourful, as well as educational, addition to any classroom.

Method

Buy a large piece of paper and draw a frame around it (for your students to decorate later). Divide the paper into twenty-six or so boxes, one for each letter of the alphabet. Clearly mark at the top of the paper "Word Chart."

Every time an unfamiliar word is encountered in class, it can be added to the chart. Write the words in small letters and very legibly—it is probably best to do this yourself. Don't forget to run through the new words at a suitable time, checking meaning, pronunciation, and so on. What a practical way of spicing up a boring wall!

Word Circle

Level: Primary 3–6

Time taken: 10 minutes

Introduction

A simple and enjoyable paper-based activity, good as a gapfiller with either individuals or groups. It can also be used to review vocabulary and spelling.

Method

For an individual or small group, use a sheet of A4 paper; for a class, use the board. Draw a circle. What is it? An egg? A football? Pizza? No—it's a word circle!

Start with an easy word, like "table," and write the word on the edge of the circle. The last letter of the word becomes the first letter of the next, chainstyle, in this case "e." The next word might be "elephants," so the next word starts with "s" and so on. Watch out—the last letter of the last word must be the same as the first letter of the first word in order to complete the circle.

Word Figure of Eight

Level: Primary 3–6

Time taken: 10 minutes

Introduction

This is similar to a Word Circle, except the template is a figure of eight. It is slightly more tricky as there is also a "cross" of letters in the middle of the "figure of eight."

Method

As with the Word Circle, use an A4 sheet for an individual or small group or the board for the whole class. Draw a large "8" and in similar fashion write the first word on the edge of the figure. So if your topic is pets the first word might be "cat," the second "turtle," the third "egg," and so on—the last letter of each word starting the next.

Be careful—there is a "cross" of letters in the middle of the figure of eight: the words coming from both directions must "cross" with the same letter.

Word Search

Level: Primary 1–6

Time taken: 10–15 minutes

Introduction

Even advanced students need to review their ABCs somehow, and this is an excellent way of doing it! The mystery of looking for hidden words conjures a strange desire in your students: the desire to work.

Method

Many commercially produced word-search books exist, but you'll have to look harder for them the farther away from the Western world you get. Why not produce some of your own? All you need is a grid of, say, twelve-by-twelve boxes. Into these boxes you can insert words related to your topic; around these words you can just write in any letters at random. The students can make such word grids for each other or simply try to solve the ones you have written.

An excellent topic for a wordsearch is the names of people in the class—it's personalized, and it shows you make the effort.

Part 5
Sample Lessons

In order to show you some of the activities in action, I have prepared four sample lessons for you. Each takes about an hour to complete. You can run through them bit by bit, or they might give you ideas for your own plans. The four lessons follow:

1. Introduction Lesson
2. Parts of the Body
3. Giving Directions
4. Going Shopping

Introduction Lesson

Level: Primary 1–6

Time taken: 1 hour

Introduction

Aimed at all levels, this one-hour lesson is both fun and practical. At the same time, it takes into account the formalities of teaching the date and taking the register (roll call).

As a general rule, first lessons can be written off as a bit of a mess. However, if you have some definite things to achieve, then the "mess" seems a little more "organized"—almost as if you planned it!

Lesson Plan

1. Introductions

    - Introduce yourself—"Good morning, Mr...."
    - Teach date (day, date, month, year)
    - Register (roll call)

2. English names

    - Names Lucky Dip
    - Ball Throw
    - Make name tags (and peg them on)

3. Vocabulary dictionary

- Preferably a separate book (can be completed for homework)

Parts of the Body

Level: Primary 1–6

Time taken: 1 hour

Introduction

Children appear to love learning about parts of the body—it seems to fill them with enthusiasm and a willingness to learn. I have taught the following lesson so many times I could almost do it with my eyes closed.

Lesson Plan

1. Formalities

- Date
- Register (roll call)

2. Presentation

- Body Annotation (stickers, as a Lucky Dip)

3. Further activities

- Simon Says
- "Head, Shoulders, Knees and Toes"
- Make a skeleton collage (handicraft)

Barry Nicholson

Giving Directions

Level: Primary 1–6

Time taken: 1 hour

Introduction

A surprising number of children, at all levels, seem to have problems distinguishing left and right. This problem must be countered! By reviewing left and right in the shape of directions, it is possible to combine a fun lesson with the solution to this problem.

Lesson Plan

1. Formalities

- Date
- Register (roll call)

2. Board presentation

- Draw three clear arrows, one pointing left, one pointing right, and one straight ahead. Drill.

3. Further activities

- Blindfold Obstacle Course
- Raise Your Left Leg
- Change!

Going Shopping

Level: Primary 1–6

Time taken: 1 hour

Introduction

Shopping is one of the more popular pastimes, and a shopping scene can easily be recreated in the classroom. Your children will enjoy the new roles they have—a taste of the real thing.

Lesson Plan

1. Formalities

- Date
- Register (roll call)

2. Presentation

- Lucky Dip (topic: shopping items)
- Drill names of items

3. Further activities

- Kim's Game
- Feel Bags
- Role Plays (topic: shop scene)

Postscript

It was almost twenty years ago that this book was first published, and it is interesting to visit it again after all this time. I remember typing it at an electric typewriter and giving the paper manuscript to the printer. How he got it into book form I haven't a clue, but, of course, these days it is a breeze to e-mail our text to whomever we want around the world. How technology has changed! And that's perhaps the main reason for the revival of this book: to get it electronically produced and brought into the contemporary age.

This book, essentially, is a straight copy of the first script printed in Hong Kong in 1996. It was written in 1995 with Hong Kong primary children in mind, but it may be applied in a range of other countries and contexts. The majority of the main text remains the same, unedited, except for typos or obvious mistakes ("pronumciation").

I like the fact that the book stresses "active," "practical," and "fun," three related items that give the book a much-needed angle rather than it just being a list or directory. It is always important to have a viewpoint rather than be purely descriptive.

With hindsight an appraisal is easier, even if it is your own work. There are some things I need to mention in retrospect. The difference in technology between then and now is obvious. Also some of the activities make me smile as my language style has altered a lot since then. For example, in the Dressing-Up Race, I tell the reader to "select a bundle of old clothes" and then to dress the children up in "floppy shirt, flowery hat, oversized shoes, and baggy trousers," somewhat suggesting that the average teacher has such clothes lying around. I, for one, do not possess a flowery hat!

Some of the "level" and "time taken" labels seem in retrospect quite random, although, as mentioned in the original, each teacher can adapt and develop the activity according to his or her own needs—lengthen it, shorten it, or put the front at the end or the end at the front.

That leads me to a final observation: the original book had no conclusion—it just ends. I should have tagged a conclusion on to the last page. That's why this postscript is added at the end now, in 2015, hopefully to conclude what I wrote back in 1995.

A new printing of this book allows me to connect with my past but in a contemporary way. It is the one and only book I have had published so far, but I certainly do not intend for it to be the last. Enjoy!

Barry Nicholson
Istanbul 2015

About the Author

Born and educated in the United Kingdom, Barry Nicholson holds a Master's degree in Teaching English as a Foreign Language from the University of Reading. During his career abroad, he has taught in the Far East, Germany, and Turkey. He currently lives and works in Istanbul.